CONFLICT
A WORLD AT WAR

EDITED BY SARAH WASHER

First published in Great Britain in 2016 by:
Forward Poetry
Remus House
Coltsfoot Drive
Peterborough
PE2 9BF

Telephone: 01733 890099
Website: www.forwardpoetry.co.uk

Book Design by Spencer Hart
© Copyright Contributors 2016
SB ISBN 978-1-84418-708-9
Printed and bound in the UK by BookPrintingUK
Website: www.bookprintinguk.com

Foreword

There are few themes that draw poets to their pens as much as the theme of war. As such a distinct element of our national and cultural identities, war reverberates through our knowledge of the past, and on into our experiences in the present day. Inspired by such a highly emotive subject, this is one of our most moving and enduring anthologies to date.

Some of the poetry in this collection focuses on the direct experience of war: the sights, sounds, smells and emotions, all blurring together to create a vivid picture in the mind's eye. Other poets explore the difficulties faced by those who are left behind, and the emotions of waiting for your loved ones to return, uncertain if they ever will.

Conflict - A World At War includes a mosaic of styles, memories and thoughts, from celebrations of heroes and elegies of remembrance to descriptions of both famous battles and personal battles through the hardships left in the wake of war.

Whichever style the poets use, or whichever emotions they evoke and pictures they create, the resounding echo left with you after reading *Conflict - A World At War* is powerful: a continuous battle for freedom, hope, and above all, a cry for peace.

Contents

The Poems

A Bouquet To Flanders

Solemnly, by a surging river she waits in solitude,
Her pale face kissed by moonlight,
Shimmering, silver wavelets dance
And sparkle in lunar radiance,
Racing impatiently towards the sea.

Alone, where once a soldier stood,
A bouquet of meadow flowers in hand,
Moist eyes glistening in moonlight,
She casts her gift upon the river,
Swiftly lost to sight,
In the dark orifice of the night.

A gentle wind wafts melancholic
Sounds across the sea,
The guns of battle,
Tidings of death and putrescent,
Faceless warriors, faithful souls,
Harvesters of death,
Across the fields of Flanders.

A solitary bouquet bobbed upon the sea,
Swept away by the running tide,
A messenger of love to a soldier,
Standing proud in freedom's fight,
Or lying, still draped in death's cloak,
Hidden beneath the dark shadows
Of the night.

Richard Kinsella

Congratulations
Richard!
Your poem has been
chosen as the best in
this collection and
you've won £25!

Respect – Ceasefire

I will follow
To the ends
Of the Earth
Lead me
To the land of plenty
Where peace dwells within
The frontline of time
I can hold on
Past the dawn
Riders in the sky
Language speaks understanding
Respect – Ceasefire!
Outside –
The military man stands alone.

S M Thompson

They Will Not Keep Us Down

They cannot keep us down,
With their bombs and guns and lies.
They cannot keep us down,
With their forms and suits and ties.
They cannot keep us down,
With their threats and hate and crimes.
They cannot keep us down,
With their rules and bans and lies.
They cannot keep us down,
We will not cower or hide,
We will not run or fear.
We will stand together, using cards and flowers.
Using children's tears, we will be strong.
We will not shout or scream,
We will stand silent and strong, in peace.

Matthew Hodder

The Veteran

We often take for granted
That old man on that chair
The one with funny clothes on
And grey, receding hair.

But if we close our eyes
Imagine who he used to be
The old man with the funny clothes on
Led a country to victory.

You never stopped to question
You only stand and judge
The old man on the park bench
Feeding ducks and eating fudge

It's once a year you see him
With his medals on display
Standing at the Cenotaph
Looking grieved and in dismay.

He stands still in reflection
In silent mourning and grief
For as the clock strikes 11
He lays down the poppy wreath.

In laying down that poppy wreath
In memory of what was -
He lost his friends and colleagues
He laid down his life for us.

Carl Onwochei

Prayer For Humanity

Prayer for humanity
In the light of your presence, Lord
Calm all our anxious fears
As we pray for *all humanity*
Through our devastated tears
Put an end to all this violence
That reigns upon our land
Remove the guns of terror
From the perpetrators' hands
In our shock, our grief and anger
Lord, be our light of hope
Through our prayers and petitions
Give us the strength to cope
Whatever race or colour, religion, faith or creed
Let us stand together
To meet each other's needs
Let our love flow through nations
As we pray for wars to cease
Fill our hearts and minds with love
As we strive for worldwide peace.

Karen Wilson

Heroes Of War

How courageous were those young men,
Not knowing if they would be coming home again.
Who in their droves signed up for war,
With belief in what they would be fighting for.

With minimal training, just not enough time,
Final farewells, heading for the front line.
Very hard moments, saying goodbyes,
Leaving loved ones, tears in eyes.

Short-lived sanctuary in those trenches,
Battle cries, screams and wartime stenches.
The orders made, obey the command
And charge the enemy, with rifle in hand.

Unrivalled bravery, those young men had shown,
Running now to desperate unknown.
With fire power lighting up the sky,
A moment in time, so many would die.

At rest now in a foreign land,
Lines of headstones proudly stand.
We owe those heroes a priceless debt,
So salute them all and never forget.

Mark Ainslie

The Battles After War

Blood on the field,
Weapons lay among the grass,
All tears have been shed,
Yet the war has yet to pass.

The battles may be over,
Yet the trauma has yet to leave,
They are heroes on the outside,
Inside there are horrors you wouldn't believe.

Our men are emotionally tortured,
They get flashbacks and sleepless nights,
They are haunted by their experiences,
All because they went to fight.

We place so much honour
On our men fighting for 'our' land,
If this is how we get them back
Do we really have the upper hand?

Nicole Phillips

Bagpipes

The bagpipes remind me of lonely places,
Of hillside and glen, of windswept moors
And solitary castles, perhaps it's that unmistakable
Sound, unique and somehow thrilling to the soul.
I saw a painting once, a brave man at war,
Piping through the storm of shot and shell,
He piped along the parapet of no-man's-land
Encouraging the hearts of scared men,
It was that sound, that unmistakable sound
Like a cat's wailing that encouraged the soldiers to
Embrace the storm and run the final lap home,
Bringing the banshee to many a window and door.

Robert W Lockett

Lambs And Guns

I am naked except for my clothes
No match for knives, bombs and gun.
You can kill me anytime you want
For my only defence is to run.

You are fully armed to your teeth
A veritable arsenal moving on legs,
So you can slaughter and maim at will
No matter how much your victim begs,
As they relax, carefree on a beach,
At a café or maybe a music hall.
Thus your foul war on the unarmed
Ensures that only the innocents fall!

Creeping, slithering, making your plans,
Hiding in shadows behind a locked door.
Disgusting cowards, strapping on bombs
For your sick, ambushing war.

Thus you avoid and won't bring to combat
Any trained and well-armed man.
So you stick to your putrid sewers
And attack, like only rats can.

I am naked except for my clothes
No match for knives, bombs and gun.
You can try to kill me anytime you want
For it's not my only defence, to run.

So stalk our free world trying to see
Easy targets like lambs, unaware, at play,
Your brainwashed mind and smoking gun
Will never earn a winner's sway.

Laurie Wilkinson

9

Do We Care?

Where did they go to, those lasses and lads
Who gave of their lives for me?
Where did they go to, those lasses and lads
So that I could simply be free?

They are sent to the places where other don't dare
Political motives no doubt
Those people that send them but don't go themselves
When the orders are just handed out

They give of their lives and their sanity too
Hoping everyone's world would improve
They do it for them, for you and for me
Being careful with each dangerous move

What care do we show those with courage like this
When they just lay their lives on the line?
Could we not do them justice, perhaps now and again
And treasure them one moment in time?

Can we send them the message now once and for all?
Whether they be at home or out there
That convinces them finally just how we feel
Let's convey to them how much we care.

James Ackland

Duncarnock Hill Fort

Whilst the west wind blaws a hardy gale
An rain fa's fast, on thon vast, open trail
E'en at times, turning water tae hail
Still, onward ah murch
Up bi Johnny's well
An under the auld arch

Under the auld arch, an o'er bi the bales
Up the auld fort, whaur yince they foun shale
An me, ah hae telt in sae mony past tales
O the brave men wha march'd
Intae battle or Hell
In a time now past

A time now past, tho fragments remain
On this ancient groun, whaur fast fa's the rain
Wi sic unwritten history; rich, in mine veins
'Twad bi sad nae tae tell
A wee tale or twa
O the men wha here fell

The men wha here fell, under emperor's reign
In an age lang ago, in a land far frae hame
In a forest covered wilderness, nae yet tamed
Fierce warriors, they did face
Wha did slay thaim a'
An sent thaim a' tae Hell or Grace

S M Ó Cuinn

11

Over The Rooftops

Over the rooftops and far away,
From all those commands I've had to obey,
Like those that ordered me to this war,
That told me to fight but not what for.

Over the rooftops and far away,
From the blood and guts that were spilled each day,
From the mustard gas, bullets and bombs,
That buried men's lives beneath the Somme.

Over the rooftops and far away,
From the screaming shells that day after day
Tortured my mind until it did crack,
They sent me on leave, I never went back.

Over the rooftops and far away,
'There he is men,' I heard one of them say,
He shouts, 'Halt in the name of the King!'
Still running, I hear their rifles sing . . .

Richard Bowdery

No Hiding

There's no hiding behind
the royal shilling,
the chain of command
and the mindless drill;
it's the hand on the gun
that does the killing,
no matter who issues
the call to kill.

Thomas Ország-Land

Oppression

I find it difficult to live
In a country that allowed,
Mark Wood to starve,
A diabetic ex-soldier to die,
And an average of 25,000 to freeze
To death each winter.

It's impossible to fathom
Why the disabled are driven
To take their own lives,
Sanctions on benefits at a whim,
It's a master plan
I don't want to be part of.

Slave wages, zero hours, food banks,
Cut taxes on multi-millionaires,
Grandparents dying on trollies,
In under-funded hospitals,
GPs that you cannot see,
MPs' expenses and corporate greed.

How sad this country is,
Taught how to hate and discriminate,
By right wing press
And a government of the rich,
For the rich and richer . . .
21st century civilisation.

How many Mark Woods,
Disabled deaths, suicides,
Do we take before
We kick down the door,
Find our conscience and say,
No way?

Norman Dickson

The Knock

His mother was in the kitchen,
There came a knock on the door,
It was a policeman with a telegram,
She buckled to the floor.

Of course she knew what it meant,
But could scarce believe it true,
Every night, she'd prayed out loud
'Lord, see him safely through.'

Her dearest boy, young and brave,
Sought glory overseas
And as he left for France she sobbed,
'Take care, come back to me.'

But her darling son isn't coming back,
He won't knock his mother's door,
He's lying in some foreign field,
Another victim of the war.

Gary Smith

The Norm

The war was prominent
for you were not
and suddenly all eyes were on me
to make money, to drag us out

That winter it snowed
your littles made snow angels
for they were one
and I paid the bills

Mother would cry
brother would smoke
I had to get money
for we were broke

My skin is stained
a canvas for predators
worth less than $30 and a cigarette
sin speaks to me

I used to make excuses
for your departure
maybe you were in debt
or just didn't want us

But now you're back
after your relaxing holiday of solitude
encompassed by whores
and forgotten family

Your shoes are shiny
your suit is creased
mother still cries
brother still smokes

You expect to walk in
to a clean kitchen
a mother who smiles
a brother who sings

But the war is still on
you stink of a whore
my body is broken
no letters, just lies

You missed a Christmas
or maybe two
who cares?
Daddy, you bastard, I'm through.

Alessia Newman

The Inheritors

Ever across the table
she sees the empty chair
and remembers the terrible deed
of Agamenmnon – the raised knife
the taut air,
the human sacrifice
of Iphigenia
- the piercing of her body
the betrayal of innocence,
token of love turned
into a political ploy.

can proles make sense of such an act
when words blown from windy Troy
replace love's tryst
with summons to slay a daughter?

The successors of Agamemnon
live in Whitehall, White House
and a thousand antiseptic offices
cleansed with rationality.
The Athenian sails
are now sheets of newsprint
blown off night presses.

Presses squeeze blood
sustained by the paparazzi
knife-poised with photo-lenses, seared with motorbikes
and endless speculation.

The goddess of love and compassion
resolves into the hunted not the huntress
dyed in blood-red and black ink.
Diana, we have become your slayer
Clytemnestra, we are your successors.

T Vanneck-Surplice

Dear Diary

Dear Diary,
Today, one of our men was found dead
Killed by a nasty blow to the head
As well as a soldier, he was a friend
When will all this madness end?
For every man there is a grave
But we have to show that we are brave
As lives end, the war still goes
When will this be over? No one knows

Dear Diary,
One of our men was shot today
He was pronounced dead and taken away
But now I suppose, that he is free
From all this pain and misery
The soldiers here seem so young
Fighting instead of having fun
But they are all so brave and strong
This is now where they belong

Dear Diary,
I'm limping, bleeding with cuts on my face
It's cold and dark, I hate this place
This war has taken so many lives
No one knows just who will survive
Every day I live in fear
That one day soon, I won't be here
I sit and wonder how I'll cope
All I can do is pray and hope

Dear Diary,
I'm sitting here in so much pain
What can all this possibly gain?
I didn't think it would be this tough
I can't take any more, I've had enough
I've tried so hard to fight this war
But I can't do this anymore
A gun to my head, I look to the sky
And one final time, I say goodbye.

Jade Bradley-Melling

For Wilfred Owen: War Poet

(' . . . From Lungs That Had Loved Laughter')

Beneath the haze of summer's
Blood-red sky, lie grey men; assembled
Yet disarrayed, their purpose destroyed
By diplomatic decisions which leave
Then as war fodder – without food,
Sleep, arms – facing death unprepared.

The bugle sounds as a death knell,
Biding aching bodies to prepare
To fight for King and Country.
What horror lies hidden beneath
Romantic recollections of such battles?
Writers sometimes tread so softly
For fear of offending
Mere mortals, who do not wish
To grasp the inhumanity of it all.

But –
How you showed what
Price men paid for the
Freedom, which we now forget we have,
With you we travel to Hell
And back, to watch these
Souls surrender sanity.

Your words like
Piercing stares penetrate
Beneath grey-shrouded
Uniforms – bruised bodies –
Sweat-soaked skin,
To sunless souls
Backed black by
Anger's heat.

Frustrations firing power paralysis
More effectively, kills the spirit
Far cleaner than gross guns
Which spill their guts across the battlefield.

When you were killed, we were
Deprived of further perfect
Word pictures to guide and
Hold us and those men
With whom you lived and died
Were left without a champion
For their cause.

Yet today, your
Tapestries of truths still
Hang within our conscience.
The soldiers' agony is caught on camera,
So we may feel and they might know
They are not forgotten.

Sue Gerrard

Sick And Tired

I'm sick of pain
And I tired of people hurting again and again

I'm sick of hate
And tired of what we create

I'm sick of suffering
And tired of the price of living

I'm sick of war
And I'm tired of wanting more

More pain
More hurt
More hate
More suffering
More war

But mostly, I'm sick and tired of this world
And I'm sick and tired of all that's being unfurled.

Rebecca Nadin

1,000 Bombers

I used to kick my tennis ball
All the way to Varndean School
With gas mask dangling round my knees
And hair dishevelled in the breeze.

One day there came a distant roar
Which made the schoolboys stand in awe
And then the noise did multiply
A thousand bombers filled the sky.

And did the airmen see us there
Waving school caps in the air?
There were no words – just deafening sound
Which filled the air and shook the ground.

Though time has passed, I still can hear
That awesome roaring in my ear
And still recall with my mind's eye
A thousand bombers passing by.

Jonathan Bryant

Let The Sunshine In

(For The Children Caught Up In War)

Put a gun in a young boy's hands
Suddenly he becomes a man
but do we really give a damn?
It's true, it's true.

To take up arms is just a sin
Fighting wars you cannot win
'Cause all he sees is suffering,
It's true, it's true.

Politicians fight this war
Sat behind their office doors
Profits made from suffering
Can't they let the sunshine in?
It's true, it's true.

They don't see the dying man
But his blood is on their hands
Is this a world we want to know?
Is this a world for a child to grow?
It's true, it's true.

A mother weeps, her body numb
For her the soldier boy is gone
His dying breaths a beating drum
It's true, it's true.

It's not her war, she's just a pawn
With no one left her world is torn
Left alone to grieve and mourn
It's true, it's true.

Watch it on the TV screen
You turn it off, return to dreams
Sitting in your comfy chair
Worlds apart, do you even care?
It's true, it's true.

It's not your kids, it's not your fight
So you can go to bed tonight,
You don't see their suffering
Can't you let the sunshine in?

So lay down your arms, let's call a truce
People of the world, that's you
Let the children have their say
Let the children go to play.

Is this a world we want to know?
Is this a world for a child to grow?
Can't we ease this suffering?
Can't we let the sunshine in?
It's true, it's true.

It's time to let the sunshine in,
It's time to end the suffering.

Trudi Mackie-Brown

Hope

Don't talk to me of man and gun,
How heroes stand and cowards run,
Don't talk to me of bombs that thud,
When hill and vale run red with blood,
Don't talk to me of lands and right,
When bargaining down rifle sights,
Don't talk to me of cannon's roar
When to me they all mean war.

Don't talk to me of man and gold,
When people starve, both young and old,
Don't talk to me of planes and cars,
When people sleep beneath the stars,
Don't talk to me of styles of hair,
When children walk with feet so bare,
Don't talk to me of who shall lead,
When to me they all mean greed.

Don't talk to me of stocks and shares,
When one mistake can cost careers,
Don't talk to me of merchandise,
When children labour for a bowl of rice,
Don't talk to me of independent rule,
When ethnic cleansing is unjust and cruel,
Don't talk to me of persecution,
When it leads to execution.

Don't talk to me of race and creed,
When bones shatter and flesh does bleed,
Don't talk to me of holy wars,
When innocents die for cause,
Don't talk to me of religious ideal,
When bodies lay beneath piles of steel,
Don't talk to me of self-sacrifice,
When life is worth not than the roll of a dice.

But talk to me of family love,
Of your Lord God and Heaven above
And talk to me of trust,
The confidence to share one's crust
And talk to me of peace on land,
With fellow man hand in hand
And talk to me of how to cope,
When to men it all means hope.

Bazil Figura

The Minister Of Modesty

In the times that we live in
It is not important that we win

We must value each other more than ever
And not think we are the most clever

Do we need a leader
Who can be the world's feeder?

We don't know what we need
Yet we sit and watch the grass of the ground bleed

A Minister of Modesty is what we require
Not some stereotypical liar

Modesty from a minister who is unharmed
Not a caged animal who has been farmed

A minister who can put himself last
But who can do this whilst forgetting the past?

Modesty in abundance would be great
One who can exhale without any hate

So I write this plea to all
For the Minister of Modesty to call

To salvage us all of our souls
And heal the deep, wounded holes.

Christine Roberts

The Unknown Soldier

Slipping away, slipping away
Have I started to lose a grip on reality?
Are we all being led astray
Thrown in a corner and forgotten
A lost dog left to go rotten?
Or are we living all year long
Helplessly drifting to a played-out song?

Locked up in a cage of your own device
Trust is an issue
Like a lonely child with a heart of ice
Disappearing within a city crowd
A dirty toy at the lost and found
Trodden so deep you should live underground

The friends I knew are long departed
Leaving me lost and left uncharted
With only a dream to make it home
And if I need to, the world I will roam
I pray for the day when I'm by your side
So I'll keep on fighting and finish the ride

There's a sinister shadow on the way
The magnitude of cries rise up to say
It's nearly my time!

Peter Pearce

I Thank You

I knew a simple soldier boy,
Whose spirit and strength shone through,
His beautiful eyes showed no fear,
He runs through the woods,
All he hears are the gunshots, the bombs,
He feels the pain in his stomach,
He hears the sounds that echo around,
His fearless heart beats with painful sobs,
He tries so hard, but cannot say a word,
He feels the pain that strikes again and again,
His eyelids feel too heavy and darkness surrounds.

He opens his eyes to see the bright, white lights,
They all want to know where he's been,
What he's seen, what he's done,
But he cannot find the words to tell them,
They couldn't imagine in their wildest dreams what he had seen,
He left knowing it would change his view on life forever,
He has seen the craziest things, felt the deepest pain,
He still stood strong and carried on,
He killed in foreign lands,
He saved the lives of many men.

They save the lives of everyone around the world,
You walk out the street, all the kids are laughing and playing,
The adults are watching, all the while gossiping,
I can't help but wonder, do they know how many people have died?
How many have lost their sight or their legs?
How much pain the bodies have been put through?
How scared they must be to sleep
Because of the memories it gives them?
Is everybody truly thankful to those that save their lives every day?
Do they realise that not every hero wears a cape or tights?
They are normal men and women who risk their lives,
Just so you can live yours,
In Flanders Fields, the poppies grow.
Between the crosses, they mark their places.

You look up and see the birds, the sun is shining,
Everything is calm, you can feel the presence of the heroes surrounding you.
They are in everyone's thoughts and dreams,
In their prayers and in their hearts.

We are free to walk down the street,
We are free to walk a corner without being afraid,
We are grateful, thank you.

Roxanne Lee

A Star-Less Sky

(In Memory Of James Henry Barnett)

Before my eyes a star-less sky
Reminiscent of a black-outed night,
I saw a red ribbon,
An unbroken silk line,
Drifting through time,
Heard the whispers turn into a scream,
Loud enough to awaken me
From my dream.
No, not a dream!
It was the nightmare again,
Pressing into my forehead,
Cold fingers, long dead,
Yet my brain felt on fire,
Burned with the words he said:

'Please write down my story,
It has to be told,
Nearly a century has passed,
But I will never grow old,
I had to leave behind all the things I held dear,
Put on the coat of bravado,
When I felt icy fear.

I was passed fit for active service,
Sent off to be trained,
Even as I was dying,
Forced to march,
Fellow soldiers had to support me on parade.

My mother, one sister could only see me through glass,
The doctor on his rounds,
Was not dressed in white,
But cloaked in black, for he diagnosed death,
Wanted me to hurry up and take my last breath,
As I lay on that bed a finger beckoned me,
To look away from the claustrophobic room,
To a hollowed out shell, mini-trench,
My awaiting, empty tomb.

Another army death was recorded,
My number, my rank,
So I could be buried in that dugout,
Dark and dank.

All the women who missed me,
Mother, sisters, daughters, my pregnant wife,
Broken-hearted, in tears,
At this bitter ending of my life,
Look at these pages,
The blanks I could never fill,
Please tell my story because no one else will,
You're my last hope,
The final link in the chain,
I'll leave it up to you, it's your choice,
To allow your pen to give me a voice,
On 3rd March, 1917, I made the ultimate sacrifice,
Met my fate,
James Henry Barnett, 8th Royal Field Artillery,
Age 28.'

Joy S J Edwards

Collateral Damage

I stagger through the maze of people torn from limb to limb,
My nostrils burn from the smoke of burning bodies within.

All around are corpses' eyes staring and mutilated hands,
Ripped from life by the rain of death,
Men, women, children dead, our bombs have hit their designated targets.

We bombed this site on military information,
But it appears we have bombed the wrong enemy station.

'Collateral damage is what I see,' is all the major can say to me,
Collateral damage but no one is caring,
We did kill at least one enemy soldier during that air raid so daring.

Gary Raymond

ISIS

An Islamic State, extremist views intolerant of the views of others,
War on the West, war in the Middle East, terrorist attacks, a holy Jihad born out of hate.
Barbaric acts against those with moderate views, atrocities against women, children and
men.
War or peace, we need to protect religious freedom from their narrow, misinterpreted view.
A new world force attacks the West, violence and terror in its most extreme, there can be no
peace in the Middle East.
We need to unite and tackle the problem of the Islamic State,
I am peace-loving, but we need to stem the tide of growing hate.

More air strikes are needed in ISIS strongholds in the Middle East,
Protect the vulnerable, protect those of differing beliefs,
Holy Jihad born out of an emerging religion meant to protect from attack, not be the
aggressor undertaking barbaric acts.
Paris, a taste of things to come and the grossest of acts against foreign lands.
War, we are given little choice against an aggressor united in hate for all.

Amanda Jayne Gilmer

The Soul Leader Of War

As the colour of your eyes disappears,
The hollow blackness reveals your unknown fear,
But is this your fear or mine?
I guess I'll find out in time.

Don't hide your eyes
Face everything and rise

If you can still smell that place of fear,
Is your own nose still there or here?
Confront me with an open heart,
To integrate your shadow part.

Then dive into the fire and rise in the sea
Empower and love yourself to accept me.

Hazel Maines

Our Heroes

You're a good man
In fact you're a hero
Every day I know you smile
Even when tears come close
You laugh despite them,
For you know there's too much sadness
And it could break you down and destroy you.

Your steel armour
But you know you're really no bullet-proof man
Sometimes it's hard to get through, just living and breathing
Other times it's even harder, a real Mission Impossible.
Whatever your days would bring
You still find a way to write a letter home
Where every word had your heart and lips sealed in it.

As before he left, his mother said,
'No one says goodbye or good luck, this is a war,
A danger field, but this is the route of life you're taking my love,'
And wept her tears away,
'See you in a little while,' this was a hopeful way of saying, 'Come back home,'
And that day, their son was a man.

And now he walked on an unbalanced lifeline
With many tears of loss
And all countries over the world shed tears, feel hurt
As they say goodbye to their war heroes
But always a war, forever the fight
But in their loved ones' eyes it isn't a good enough reason to have to say goodbye
For all the years and generations there still is war
But still, with our love and grace
We send thanks to our heroes
Every one of them, for every day that they walk the lifeline of war.

Danielle Harris

War

War
The never-ending struggle
Of man versus man
So endless and futile

War
Fighting for lord
Fighting for land
Fighting for the sake of fighting

War
Death is constant
Lives cut short
Nothing is gained

War
Is obsolete
Is mindless
Is meaningless

War
Of the body
Of the mind
Of our very emotions

War
Will always be there
Will always be coming
Will continue until the last human is gone.

Patrick Rowe

War!

The battle
fought over nothing
but space.
Endless race
of time and ending
of life.
Bodies galore
scattered all over
the battlefield
wasted energy.
Blood and guts.
Bleeding bits.
Death in the air.
Totally pointless
ending of worlds
ending of people
ending of future life.
Bullets and missiles
flying rapidly, everywhere.
Powers that be
controlling the future outcome.
People power.
Revelation to succeed against
dictatorship.
War is no good at all.

Andrew Hinds

Crisis In The Middle East And Around The World

Chaos now threatens the world,
It is paramount we take appropriate action
And eradicate the tit-for-tat mentality sooner than later.
The free world is enraged by Isil and other known terrorist groups,
Who have waged war upon innocent men, women and children,
All because of their beliefs, who are hell-bent on retaliation.
It's diabolical to say the least, the suffering that is being caused.
All in the name of Islam, by cruel, inhuman gunmen
Who cite the Quran as factual, but in reality is a
Misrepresentation of its reading and script.
It is now a downward spiral of murderous actions
By Daesh. War is not profitable, it is destructive in
All of its forms, which are disgusting, which merit no gain.
The world must unite against this evil terror and help
Those most affected, whatever creed, race or colour.
The world needs democracy and equality more than ever
And rid Syria and Iraq of the enemy within.
Down with Isil's murderous regime and all that it stands for.
War is the hater of Mankind and always will be,
With pure hatred in its ranks.
Philosophically speaking the reality is demonstrated
By their lack of human tolerance, those who behead, torture,
Those who bring devastation and fear to the Middle East,
Africa and Europe
Which is sinister, dark and evil in all of its contents.
ISIS, AL Qaeda, Al Shahab, Boko Haram, the main culprits
A melting pot of radicalised extremist
Whose tentacles reach around the world,
Blowing up innocent people and destroying beautiful ancient buildings.
We only have to look around the world
And we see that democracy and equality works,
Where, in the east continent, radical beliefs do not work.
We now seem to be in a fearful position
We are damned if we do and damned if we don't take
Moderate action and rid the world of this evil menace
Once and for all. I fear the Russians are now making things worse
By bombing innocent targets, we all know the Russians do not mess

About. Look what happened in Afghanistan and previous to that in Vietnam, we lost the
momentum in bringing total victory,
Against an inferior enemy.
We must never let the disciples of terror win this time around.
It is inevitable that we need to put troops on the ground,
In Northern Syria and Iraq and drive out the regimes
Responsible for wholesale slaughter, we cannot rely
On bombing the enemy alone, too many innocent lives
Are being lost daily, one life is too many.
We must force the evil antagonists from their strongholds
And eradicate them before the world fails in its duty
To protect our beautiful human beings and cities.
God must be enraged by all of this wickedness,
For He gave us free will and a beautiful world to live in
And what happens is that extremists decide to destroy
Everything that is precious to law-abiding citizens.
Our children and women are frightened by all
Of this mayhem and murder which has now reached
Epidemic proportions. Love must prevail over evil doctrines,
For love conquers all eventually.

James S Cameron

The Two Gladiators In Combat In Rome

Stepping silently onto the chosen place
Both being grave-faced
With the hate blazing in their eyes
Both with teeth and sweating brows
Swords held firm, taking control of power
Fighting a battle in which one must without a doubt end his young life
And knowing that their tomorrow may never come.

The swords, slashing, lashing with brutal force
Desperate to live, yet wanting to die just to hear
The victorious, triumphant cries
Crowds roaring, thunderous applause!
Waiting until death takes its course.

Sammy Michael Davis

War!

What is it with this world today we seemed obsessed with war, but what I'd like to know is, what are we fighting for?

I just cannot comprehend what wars set out to achieve, all that seems apparent is the death and destruction they all leave.

Many lives are lost and horrific injuries sustained, but when all is said and done have their efforts been in vain?

It must be truly awful for all the families left at home, there's nothing they can do but wait for them to phone.

I have the utmost respect for all our service men and women who fearlessly fight on and hope that they are winning.

If it wasn't for these heroes who defend our foreign shores, the life we're all accustomed to would not be anymore.

No matter what you think of war it's been the same for generations, in fact it's always been the case for each and every nation.

Maybe in the future these conflicts will all end and the world will live together and be the best of friends.

I hope and pray that day comes soon when fighting will all cease, and then all God's precious children will live their lives in peace.

Catherine Wilson

Muslim

Morning light shines on my face,
permitting me to see the true colour of my race.
I draw myself to rise in my veil, my burka and face
the dreadful truths about the devilish Daesh.

Underneath my search for answers, I descend into darkness
and with open arms the traitors of Islam call us.
They say 'You are against us'
and 'I and you are the witness.'
So 'Join us and become fearsome and fearless.'
I do know of the hate crimes against our men, women and their brood,
but is this not the evils of the world who wrongly intrude.
They will rightly face their judgement on that very day
and will not be able to face the price of punishment they will have to pay.

Sorry I say, I repeatedly apologise for something I did not do,
for something I had no power over, for something I could not undo.
To the never-ending innocent bloodstream I see, I cry, I scream.
I begin to walk with my head down and do not meet anyone's eye,
I have removed myself from my community as they see me as part of the lie.

'Loved ones are attacked because of their veils, join us, we care for you,' they say,
'we will fight together, brother and sister, come on, obey,
They do not see you for who you are, they seize your hand for you to stay.
But I know you will deceive me, I know you will lie
and in your world war leave me and you to die.
I know I will not join you, I will so rightly turn away,
to hide and hate you for the image you have portrayed.

ISIS they call themselves when they do not represent Islam.
Do not leave your cradling mother's arms as your Heaven lies beneath her feet.
Do not leave your father as your duties to him will remain incomplete.
Do not leave your crying brood as they need your guidance to defeat
the inner demonic whispers that have led but a few to a path of deceit.

Murder scenes on the news and the evil slaughters carry my name.
The world hears condemning and crying out that you are all to blame.
I pray to my Lord to give us patience, I pray to my Lord to give us peace
and for this violent, vulgarised vengeance to cease.
And to end my prayer I say
'I am a Muslim, my religion is proudly Islam
Allah is the Lord and His word is the glorious Quran.'

Noreen Malik

Brave Are The Few

She had waited a long time
For a ring of bright diamonds
Telling the whole world
What she already knew
He smiled at her sweetly
Slipped the ring on her finger
Then was gone in a moment
To join the rest of his crew

He was one of a unit
A close band of brothers
Fighting a battle
In a land far away
In a featureless desert
Under hot sun and dry sand
Never quite knowing
If it's your turn today

It is said that you don't hear
The bullet that finds you
Out in the desert
Amid the affray
But it hit like a hammer
And felt like a car crash
And his captain said, tearfully
'Son, you'll be OK'

He died in the desert
In the cool of the evening
While the boys won the skirmish
It happens that way
They carried him gently
Back to headquarters
Where an aircraft stood waiting
His flight home to UK

She had waited a long time
For a ring of bright diamonds
Telling the whole world
What she already knew
He appeared to her briefly
For one fleeting moment
And as he died in the desert
She already knew

The diamonds they sparkled
In the sunshine in chapel
The service was poignant
It spoke of his life
Her eyes filled with teardrops
Like those bright, sparkling diamonds
Whilst growing inside her
Was a tiny new life!

He was one of a unit
A close band of brothers
Living and dying
So brave are the few.

David K Wilson

Your Country Needs You

I want to join the army, I want to go to war
Don't care whose side I end up on or what I'm fighting for
They'll write a song about me, the ones whose lives I save
How I was such a hero, how I was really brave
I didn't stop to question the reason for the fight
It matters not a jot to me which side was wrong or right
I'd checked of course, before I joined and details I had found
Important things that meant a lot, the rupee or the pound
I guess I like the uniform and comrades who are fun
I guess I like the way of life, I guess I like the gun
They say the conflict will be long and neither side can win
My bank will sort out my estate, I'll email them with my pin
Another day unfolds itself as through our trench I crawl
Remember not to raise my head, survival is my rule
But what is this? I sense a trap, a landmine hidden deep
Confusion reigns, the land explodes and soon I fall asleep
And when I awake, with tired eyes and search the walls and floor
I realise I'd had a dream and do not want to go to war.

Graham Hayden

The Casualty Of Youth

Are we not beasts?
Do we never tire from the killing and slaughter of innocents?
Sent to foreign shores
For parliaments grey men
Lusting for power and greed
At the flick of a pen
The doomed youth of Owens' plea
Generations pass, the story never ends
Left shattered, broken
Screaming nights
Damaged minds and bodies
Sleeping rough
War forgotten in a bottle or a fix
Why go on with this folly?
Youth closed under coffin lids
Never forget their sacrifice
They still answer the call
Lambs to the slaughter
How many more have to fall?
Remember those who are gone
Their futures no more
Care for those left
Their mind has no peace
Drunken in doorways
Locked in prison cells
The casualties grow
Battlefields continued in suicide's throw.

W.S. Elliott

For The Children

We want a world where children walk
In peace and free from fear.
A world where mothers know for sure
What family they will rear.
Let fathers know their tools of trade
Are not the gunman's rod,
Where people of both sides
Unite in peace with God.

Our days are full of sorrow
And we can only say
What we want for tomorrow
Is a peaceful, bloodless day.
It is so hard for those who lost
Their loved ones in the fray.
But teach us now to show them Lord
Your love in every way.

Babies lie in pools of blood,
Their coffins tell the tale.
Of families who are slaughtered
In a senseless, blood-filled way.
When lives are shattered, just to prove,
Who will not give in first.
But Lord let us make the move
And listen to our prayers.

For now our hearts are crying Lord,
for those across the sea,
let the hatred and the deathly cloud
be beaten by their love for Thee.
while leaders meet to talk,
oh Lord, this is our prayer.
Let mothers, fathers, children walk
in peace and goodwill on Earth.
Brenda Longstaffe-Smith

When Will It End?

When will it end; the days we open our emails and find we have lost another friend?
After yet another day's dawning there is yet another day's mourning,
People we served with, now dying younger and younger, not by famine, not by hunger.

When will it end; our soldiers sleeping rough on the street,
the politicians find the covenant hard to meet?
Soldiers with PTSD, treated badly on Civvy Street,
if we weren't so macho we would breakdown and greet,
Left alone to our devices, some succumb to drink and drugs or any of the available vices.

When will it end; that time we no longer hear from the battlefield
of a fallen warrior and friend?
Soldiers told that they are no longer wanted as the TA are told to take the strain, will their
sacrifice all be in vain?
Soldiers toil and suffer on the battlefield in a war from another age, but it's time they
received a decent wage.

When will it end; that we treat our veterans like cast-offs and flunkies, but bend over
backwards for scroungers and junkies?
Will the politicians wake up and realise our soldiers are in harm's way or are they more
concerned with the rules they choose to bend?

We served out country, we did our best, but as a wise man once said,
'The measure of how a country treats its armed forces is the ultimate test.'

Tom Murray

Beneath French Farms

Beneath French farms
stiff oaks under blankets, grey
unfold,
reclaimed by old Madame, staring,
cold.
Bold, bare veins sway in Winter's blow,
slicing through heads, snarc falling snow,
flaked layers rest on wilt leaded crops.
Grown where mown hearts ceased to beat,
bloodied Summer blooms now shoot
above still feet,
beneath French farms.

In the same bloody mud lost that March,
march scared witless, wilting privates,
shell-shocked,
soiled and scarred.
Bayonets, keen as mustard smog, up to dank knees in putrid bogs,
silhouetted phantoms, the eternal guard.
'Fall out!'
Ruby-lipped Mademoiselles wait
to bathe the privates' soiled privates . . .
not today . . .
Today the RSM's bark booms orders through the fog –
'Fall in!'
Must go again . . . the whistle peeps
and again
and again
to gain that yard . . .
No captain to lead, his voice-box withered, charred . . .
by bomb shard lead.
He fell dead
on steep clay,
last sneering words,
'Tosh to the Bosch!'
Now moulded
in the same bloody mud they lost that March.

Still, mithered men stand to, en garde . . .
old wounds scratched by the plough of Jean Claude.
Unearthed pocket book,
leather crinkled, worm worn,
sepia snapped sweetheart, faded and torn.
No Spring Somme sun or skylarks' song
can drown whispering English tongues,
swollen, blistered lips,
green gassed gills,
of fathers, husbands,
brothers, beaus and sons, who
lie stiff – where they fell,
shoulder to shoulder,
still talking over the village cemetery bell,
still talking of squeezes and teases, from lasses with cleavage,
still talking
of warm-welcome arms, cold pints, beef barms . . .
the day of returning
from beneath French farms.

Steve Douglas

No-Man's-Land

Where houses stood,
Crumbled walls now mark out rooms
Where laughter thrived.

A quiet woodland glade,
Now smoking stumps like rotten teeth
Rise from the blackened earth.

In lazy flower meads
Where cattle grazed,
Bloated carcasses now putrefy
The heavy, stagnant air.

Where peace once reigned,
A godless hell now stalks the land
And smiles upon its victory.

And young men,
Tall and strong,
Fall like rain upon the earth.

Bob Harris

War Or Duty?

Modern-day Saracens undertaking a holy war
Jihadist warriors spilling the infidels' blood
Retribution they've long waited for
Devout, holy disciples forsaking the sanctity of life
Not caring how they achieve their aims
Bullet, bomb or knife!
Devotees hasten to join this unholy brigade
All dressed in black for martyrdom
Terrorists on parade
Extremists eager to achieve the ultimate sacrifice
Gaining immediate entry into Islamic paradise
Preached Hadith's of uncertain authenticity
Instilling hate by deliberate duplicity
Trained by leaders with merciless affiliations
Practising brainwashing violent indoctrinations
Fundamentalists' religious wars
All fought in deepest vain
Dying for tyrants with their own political aims
Conceived in the name of Allah
Massacre, torture and public execution of all the unbelievers
Mujahedeen tricked into atrocities
A Fatwa issued by ruthless deceivers.

Paula Holdstock

1915

24th December 1915, sitting in a dark, cold and icy trench
British soldiers tired and weary from a long and bloody battlement
Yet in the distance, not too far away, carried by the night air
Familiar sounds of a Christmas carol sung by the German soldiers
The British soldiers, hearing this, respond with mirth and haste
With a united rendition of 'Good King Wenceslas'
Silence falls once more upon the trenches till the break of dawn
Christmas Day, peace on Earth for every man, woman and child born

Banter breaks out between the trenches; shouting and laughter from all the men
British soldiers scramble up the trench to be greeted by Germans with merriment
More British and German soldiers from the trenches meet in no-man's-land
Greeting each other with smiles and laughter and a shaking of the hand
A football is produced from out of the blue, to the men's cheer and delight
A game is played, with no winners or losers, everyone is happy and bright
With laughter and merriment, the game continues for thirty minutes or more
Until the truce ends when a British Major sent the British soldiers back with an order!

The British soldiers sent back to the trench where it was cold, dank and grim
The Major reminds the soldiers *'they are there to kill the Hun and not make friends with him'*
The Christmas truce was shortly lived, soldiers ready now to fire at their newly made friends
Friends made of young men just like them, now back to being their enemy once again
The sound of banter and singing now replaced with firing artillery
The sound of laughter now replaced with wounded soldiers' pain and misery
For the lives lost of so many men, their families grieved and wept
Remembering the fallen soldiers one hundred years on – lest we forget.

Sarah Louise Franks

The Tragedy Of War

War rips and tears the emotions
Sad, unhappy thoughts, mental commotions
The demons in the mind so unkind
As dark thoughts of war unveil, unwind

Yet the light is bright in the soul
As war loosens the grip on mortal control
In a time of dark shadows of doom
Life in the trenches is a living tomb

Thoughts of home brightly shine
And all loved ones are images in the mind
Sadness of the heart is an internal war
But melancholy thoughts will be left behind

The heart needs purer dreams to possess
But war awakes an all-consuming Hell
In the fiery furnace doom and death oppress
Deathly cries echo in the din of exploding shells

The landscape has no resplendence to behold
It is the bugle's echo that inflames them all
The high-pitched wailing, the deathly call
As comrades and brothers, wounded or dead, fall

No weary mind can escape the battle's surge
Rolls of men like the tide swirl and crawl
Called to fight they hear shells and bullets sing
The cold kiss of death smashes bone, tears skin

Bayonets fixed, the killing turns minutes into hours
Death will soon be replaced by mournful poppy flowers
The repentance for killing will come in later years
And the remembrance of war, the source of many tears.

James Tracey-Burner

ISIS

Whether Christian, Jew
Muslim or Hindu
Do you think he will differentiate?
When he wants to shoot me or you?
We need to break them down
And not between us frown
As the innocent here we hate
We will seal our own fate
And give them what they want on a plate.
For when we blame and argue
They quietly find a way through.
Firing back, they will not stop
But the innocent population will surely drop.
Words of love, truth, faith and humanity
May open their hearts to be free
And minds brainwashed, they will see.
Their intentions they will fail to achieve
That as humans we naturally believe;
Strength in numbers, goodness and dedication
May make them think and fall back
Instil fear and hesitation
Rather than stand to attack
It may cause a distraction
And correct the misinterpretation
To drop their arms and
Result in Godly inspiration.

But we need to take action
To stop this destruction
And see real, positive progression
We need to be together
And trust one another
Let's combine our motivation
Ignore political contradiction
To be united, a community
Not just in faith or religion
But the army of humanity
Shoulder to shoulder
Treating each other with dignity

To show evil that we are better
With no fear of mortality

For the Mahdi (Saviour)
We are waiting patiently
Isn't he awaiting the hour
When we will be ready?

The media may brand Muslims
As terrorists, but are we?
The ignorant have labelled
Us to be such people
Then let us show the world
Let's please God and show the Saviour
That we can be true ISIS
But not the knife-wielding monsters
Rather the defenders of who?
Not just our brothers, but sisters too
In faith, religion and humanity through
Let's show them the ISIS that
Our religion allows us to be
Which is just simply:
Inspirational Souls In Society.

Abbas Hooda

Fated

An eye for an eye -
the first ripped out
mercilessly, carved clean
from the socket by the
much sought after tooth,
whose legacy is one of
silver and sugar-coating.

Abigail Staniforth

The Unknown Traveller (The Afterwar Soldier)

(In Our Grandfather's Memory)

Unknown traveller . . .

From where are you coming? You have forgotten
and your name, don't want to remember anymore
in this dark age you chose path thorny
with no destination

You put your hand in jacket
and you find soil
pictures and memories filled with dust
moments which in past ages were travelling you
as the snow does

- Unknown traveller . . .

In the crossroad of your life
you chose tears again
refused to become eagle
in a sky full of mud

There that times led you
you want now to seek
and change
your lifetime journey

But the same thought that brought you here
now it drives you away . . .

Long and increasingly further away
in a wandering soul-journey that never ends . . .

Antonios Saragkas

When The War Is Over

I know everything is just too much
Trying to always hang onto my dream and your every truthful
Word, as I make my way in this crowded world of wars
Even when things get cold and we don't see eye to eye
I never lose faith
All we have is love and when we run out of food, we can still see a better day
This is not the end, we can make it through and
You always bring me back home, offering
Shelter and protection from my enemies
And a safe place to recover from all the anxieties in this mad world
We both belong together and this grave situation will make us stronger, like heroes
We will see our names printed in every newspaper when the war is finally over
Even if we are torn apart, like in a storm, we will survive the worst of days
Battling it through icy weather with only old clothes to cover the healing scars
While bombs are thrown in the night. In this Blitz
Even in our darkest depths, like windblown refugees
We hold onto each other's hand and pray in our moments of solitary confinement
Great despair and anguish, for the pain to go away!
So I am left alone, to put all my blame on this cold war
That has destroyed our family and driven some people insane.
Being the brave one, I have no time or room for regret and sorrow
So I pack my things if I am lucky to survive, like some others before me
And move on to a better day, where love and trust is the only thing left for us to build upon
When the war ends.
Then changes are inevitable, when world leaders come together
To support peace again.

Nassira Ouadi

This Angry World

Come the paling of the moon and the rising of the sun,
The ebbing and the swelling of the tides,
Someplace, somewhere a war goes on,
Pandemonium spread worldwide.
The demons of battle, their wrath and ire,
That thrive on blood, sweat and tears,
Death and destruction and smoke and fire
Seeking the elusive, they fight for peace.
The harmonies to answer the cause,
That magic ingredient beyond our reach to quell all raging wars.
Come the rising of the moon and the setting of the sun,
To the tides that ebb and swell,
Someplace, somewhere, still raging on,
A war's being fought right now.
Their seeds are sown deeply about,
If this world was a place of love and peace
Mankind would invent it, no doubt.

Peter Terence Ridgway

A Soldier's Poem

At a friend's house in the country
I met a beautiful young lady,
As the day was hot and humid
We left our friend playing tennis
And wandered down country lanes
Passing rippling fields of corn.
Her perfume became intoxicating
As we lay down in the long meadow grass
We kissed, staying there for hours.
In the evening we strolled along the Thames,
Drinking wine on a terrace overlooking the river
Making the most of the time we had left together.
At Victoria Station, there were hundreds of young men
Saying goodbye to mothers and girlfriends,
They were singing the song, 'It's A Long Way To Tipperary'
Before the war, they had been postmen, shop assistants, clerks
I heard someone say it will be a lark leaving Dover
We need to get there before this war is over.
It's Saturday, the 1st of July 1916, seven thirty in the morning
The Battle of the Somme has just begun
Whistles are blown, we all move forward,
Shoulder to shoulder, line after line,
Walking towards enemy gunfire.
The battlefield was full of shell holes and barbed wire,
Shells crashing, a hail of gunfire over our heads,
Machine guns stuttered, there was smoke and dust everywhere.
We kept moving as parts of men flew through the air,
The bombardment failed, yet we still moved forward
Men cut down like a scythe slicing through grass.
Screams of agony all around, as we crossed the pitted landscape
I found it hard to believe I was still alive,
My comrades lay on barbed wires, their bodies jerking, twisted, crucified
The rats around us as big as cats, living of the corpses of the dead
Scattered all around in the hazy sunlight.
A black cloud of flies descend as day becomes night
The captain blew his whistle, 'Bayonets at the ready'
We climbed out of the trench, the dead and dying
Lay so thick they looked like sleeping sheep,
I lay on one poor chap, he begged me for help

But I had to leave him and carry on
You couldn't stay too long out in the open.
The dead ran into tens of thousands
Bodies stacked like firewood
Others were mutilated, blinded, choking their lives away,
I stopped for a comrade, 'Keep going,' the captain shouted,
Two of his fingers had been blown off,
I knew him, he was a friend of my brother's
He was hysterical, screaming for his mother,
I tried pulling him out of the line of fire
Suddenly pain and the sky went black.
The next thing I knew, I was at Victoria Station
Doctors and nurses seeing to the injured
My right leg was covered in bandages
The pain was excruciating.
'You still have shrapnel in there son'
Said a doctor rushing over
'But, with any luck you won't lose it
For you the war is over'
Even though I'm wounded
I'm one of the lucky ones
My family, friends and the girl I love
Will be waiting at the end of my journey.

Sandra P Wood

The Bank

The line between the 1930s and the 1940s is blurred now,
A faded memory of a rose-tinted time,
Blurred not only by time, but by fiery orange-black streaks of dreadful desolation.

Even Lloyds, once prosperous and pristine in white stone
Is unglamorous as an air raid shelter.
If only the image was a film;
A hidden projectionist could spin back the flickering images,
The signs would repair themselves, become clean,
Back to the glamour of an Art Deco world.

Now, in 2015, Britain has regained its shine, despite endless cuts,
However, the shininess is different;
As we strive for corporate perfection fuelled by greed,
The labour that once made this country gleam is gone.
Just like the bank and the café next door – Deller's.
Almost ironic that the roofs were ripped off by bombs. Who was to know
That just months later
The buildings would follow?

If only the world had stopped in '38,
Britain's aesthetic would not now be so nostalgic.
But in 1939, war took men as it had before,
As a now scarcely imaginable bomb removed the signs,
Brought down dust in the streets
And smashed windows and lives.

While Britain rebuilt its way of life,
The wet cement is not yet dry on a wall that will divide
Two halves of a country.
A wall that changed the face of Germany,
For almost thirty years.
Whilst men landed on the moon,
Colour film improved; the wall became coloured by graffiti,
Digital watches appeared,
Finally the Internet was invented the year before it fell.
Then it fell.

And though the memories haven't gone –
The wall has
And the space has changed;
The cobbles have had tarmac slapped on, the streets are painted,
The builders are long gone.
Conflict is over,
But the wound still hasn't healed.

Edward Rouse

Bloody Taylor (A Fallen Soldier)

Listen to the shells dropping to the ground
Watch the enemies fall down
The sound is enough to make you mad
I was just an ordinary dad fighting for my territories
What makes me so angry, is that they say
I had blood on my hands killing another man
But that was part of the plan
I never saw my children grow up
I was blown to pieces inside a truck
I never did make it back home
I'm now just a luggage of bones
I know the officials got my wife on the phone
I don't really want anybody looking after what's my own
The situation couldn't be controlled
I had to play a role
The impact of the explosion took its toll and let's say I never woke
I used to fantasise what it would be like 'on the line' as a child
Me and my friends used to reminisce about planes coming out of the sky
We used to say it was us flying at the time
It ain't no laughing joke when you see people like yourselves
Losing limbs and their sight
We often get traumatised, waking up with cold sweats at night
Thinking you're dying
I guess we don't realise the full extent until it bites
I've lost my life
Others will find they're losing their minds
We can't leave memories behind
Sometimes we'd be patrolling derelicts where there's no light
Despite all the equipment we still need to open our eyes
In the sunshine where the spectrum blinds
We always have to look out for the danger signs
We're always seeing rats and mice underneath pipes
Remember, back in the day, the food was never any good
We used to lack nutrients which was unpleasant
Deficiency was and still is detrimental
We didn't have the lavish ingredients
Now we get efficient cooks
The smell is quite heaven sent
It's the closest we're going to get to a Christmas dinner

Shame there's no straight-out-of-the-refrigerator lagers
It's what the other lads have in favour
It's not right to get drunk on the job
But we need something also festive to wash down all that nosh
If we're lucky enough, we could be supplied with Coca-Cola
It's up-my-street type of drink
Full works with all the trimmings
I wonder what's for sweet
Mmm . . . mince pies with cream
For a minute, all seems jolly with a bit of holly
But the real pain can never go away
We will be commemorating on that day
But nothing will change
The war has been going on and on
The men are going out there 'cause they want to be thought of as strong
Worn down by pounds of bombs 'cause you don't know where
The next grenade will be coming from
Obviously the enemies had done wrong
We've got to be agile
Minutes they could be there
The next they could be gone
It's a matter of how long
It's not nice having children get caught in the crossfire
Those children could have been mine
We were trained so young how to handle guns
We take it in our stride to see blood
And the effect it has on us
We see the red stuff so much, we don't even feel numb
It's all about the adrenaline rush
Some don't see the fuss they'll shoot anyone
How come?
Well they're just doing it for a bit of fun
Things will start to get serious when they get hit by slugs
It's another family losing their son
It's another family losing a child
It's another family losing cousins
It's another family losing husbands
It's another family losing nephews
It's another family losing uncles
It's another family losing friends
It's another family losing boyfriends

It's another family losing brothers
It's another family losing fathers
It's another family losing grandfathers

Peace to the husbands
Peace to the cousins
Peace to the sons
Peace to the nephews
Peace to the uncles
Peace to the brothers
Peace to the grandfathers
Peace to the fathers
Peace to the friends
Peace to the boyfriends . . . let's all rip!

Natalie Peterson

Women At War

They condemned her for treason;
that was the reason they gave
to kill the nurse whose compassion saved
soldiers, regardless of their nationality.
A woman of integrity and loyalty
to those in need, to those she freed.
For Edith Cavell, patriotism wasn't enough;
she died with forgiveness,
she died with love.
A life lost, for a future found.

They condemned her for spying;
it was the reason they gave
for her dying.
Violette's optimism inspired others.
Her strength to resist
was brutally punished by the Fascists
who took away her life.
The life that she had,
was all that she had.
A life lost, for a future found.

Mary Chapman

One Click And It's Gone

Remembering school days
in terms of colour
it has to be blue.

The sky, my uniform
and the blossom bells
on our jacaranda trees
which,
in summer's heat
fell to the ground.

We raced around
the schoolyard
stomping and popping
the bells,
kicking and tossing
them into heaps.
If their stickiness
touched our eyes
it gave us pink-eye.

Now,
only one tree remains.
School a burnt ruin
the children gone.

Zueila is calling.

I touch the screen
my tears falling,
as I close down
my satellite eyes.
The past
slowly disappears
into the vastness of Africa.

My Zuelia loves snow.
Gillian White

Life's Battlefield

Take the blame and go on living,
feel the shame but don't give up,
know the weight of heavy burdens,
taste the salted, bitter cup.

Now reopened, old wound bleeding,
weakening every step you take,
slowly, grimly, so tenacious,
cling to effort – though you break.

Even shots from dying soldiers
help to keep the foe at bay.
Look with glazing eyes – so mortal –
to the breaking of God's day.

Through the sting of thrusting arrows,
feel your own sword turn on you,
touch the hem of Healing's garment,
feel God's peace as it flows through.

Keep your eyes upon the target
and your prize within God's grasp.
He will guide you through the quagmire
To the welcome of his clasp.

Doris R Townsend

World At War

IRA and ISIS are terrorists
They give religion a bad name
They tear us apart
They destroy everything in their path
While spreading anger, fear and pain.

Don't invade
Don't plant the seeds of vengeance and hate
Seek peace, not hate
Don't make the same mistake
By turning to guns and bombs
Stop the destruction
Act with compassion
Don't commit another wrong

Her tears have dried
She cried all night
She lost the ones she loved
There is nobody to hug her
Say it will get better
Nobody to give her hope

We all seek His protection
We are all His creation
No matter what our religion or race
We have no right
To take the life
Of those we think we hate

It's my world, it's your world
Let love unfold
Let's protect it with all our might
Let's walk the distance
Let's be persistent
Let's end this terrible fight

A war does not solve anything
It only leads to misunderstanding
Between the countries involved
It creates divisions, friction and aggression
Problems are never resolved

Fix the damage and start to create
A better life before it's too late . . .

Helen N A Choudhury

Machine Guns For Goalposts

Behind brave faces there lies despair
By the grave, allies and enemies share,
Where goodwill to all men and peace is rare
Life goes on but death is everywhere.

Bodies of men lie where poppies grew
And along with them their dreams die too,
But today angels fly where bullets flew
In the clear skies above this rendezvous.

For one day their differences are put aside
The gates of Hell shut and both sides are allied,
In the rivers of blood and mountains of mud
Where the victims of war heroically stood.

In the battlefield, which today, became the field of play
For the beautiful game on Christmas Day,
The fathers and sons, soon to be ghosts
Laid down their machine guns as goalposts.

And in Hell's playground of bullets and barbed wire
The rarely found common ground of peace they desire,
Is drowned out by the sound of shells and gunfire
Until Christmas bells ring and bring out the choir.

And in the name and spirit of Christmas they meet
To claim a victory for peace in a war of defeat,
The dying flame of humanity, not yet obsolete
As today they sing from the same hymn sheet.

And as their Christmas carols fill the air
The many smoking barrels of warfare,
Fall silent as soldiers unite in prayer
For an end in sight of every crosshair.

And with hope in their hearts they are guided
To be united by peace in a world divided,
Sparing thoughts for all the lives cut short
Sharing Christmas with the men they fought.

As they join together in subdued celebrations
This Christmas truce, is the smallest of consolations,
For these men of different nations and generations
Are all brothers in arms, not so distant relations.

Stuart Brisco

The New World

After the nuclear war ended,
there were two tribes, Kargs and Abels,
society was Third World level,
it was a London run by the Abels,
the Kargs were warlike,
the Abels ran London,
trade was done by selling mobiles,
mobiles were the currency.

We ate all the food, (rats and mice),
no crops are in the fields,
the ground is sterile,
no cows, no sheep,
the mutants, they are all around,
the monstrously deformed Kargs.

The Kargs are mostly mutants,
some more human, some deformed,
the trade is done by selling mobiles.

Looking at the reconstruction,
a brand new age of Kargs and Abels.
The New World.

Christopher Gillham

My Brother

Left with nothing
Too trapped in a war to be at peace
Too damaged to be at war
For all those soldiers, think
'For those I love, I will sacrifice'
You have sacrificed
To constantly feel at war with yourself
Because in a war
There are no unwounded soldiers
You do not know your existence gives hope
Can you not wear your tragedies as armour
Instead of being shackled to the spot
As the world goes by
Too fast and too loud
Too blurry and too painful?
So if you let us in
We promise not to break anything
For a wounded soldier may look strong
But his foundation will shake
You, my brother, are a hero
Even though you relive your moments in your nightmares.

Heather Jane Edwards

The Third World War 2037-2039

The question asked – what is your view on war?

First World War soldiers suffered discomfort,
Waiting in muddy, rat-infested trenches,
To emerge over the top, into Hell.
There they face artillery, grenades, guns,
Mines, poison gas, shells and the Grim Reaper.
When the horrific war dragged to its end,
It was declared the war to end all wars,
But that was a lie, as war followed war.
Across one hundred and twenty-five years
Technology revolutionised war.

Second World War weapons were only worse,
Advanced machine guns to increase kills.
Aircraft developed beyond recognition,
Meant bombs raining down to kill civilians.
Atom bombs caused genocide in Japan,
Londoners slept in Underground stations,
While bombs pummelled homes to heaps of rubble.
This repeated, in towns around the world,
With loved ones killed in battles and Blitzkreig,
No family unaffected by the loss.

The Third World War was different again,
All satellites were zapped by laser beams,
Demolishing world communication.
Chemical bombs destroyed soil for growing,
Electricity supplies were targets,
When the nuclear power stations were bombed.
Populations died as radiation spread,
To defeat their enemies' objective,
Oil states destroyed or burnt every field,
Any normal life was impossible.

The Third World War certainly proved to be
By destruction, the war to end all wars.
What always caused wars? In just one word – greed!
Claims to territory or possessions,
But now there is nothing left to fight for.
The First World War killed at least ten million soldiers,

Wartime disease killed seven million civilians.
The Second World War killed eighty million people,
Including some fifty-five million civilians.
World War three killed countless millions
And counting . . .

My views on war are plain, in one word, It's obscene!

Julie Freeborn

The Soldier's Tail

The ground shakes under 10,000 feet
Reality hits them and their hearts skip a beat
But they fight for their country, a country held dear
So her golden eagle quells their fear

A mass of blue advancing steady
Towards a horizon of red, nervous but ready
The man-made hammer brought forward by drumming
But the thin line of Redcoats know what's coming

At 100 yards the muskets rise
With the orders to wait for the whites of their eyes
But the French don't falter as morale's at its height
With bayonets ready, they're ready to fight

With white eyes in view, muskets are primed
Sergeants roar, the order perfectly timed
Along the British line a wave of smoke
And the Redcoats are hidden in war's natural cloak

Blue-coated bodies fall face down in mud
Unused muskets encrusted in blood
Countrymen step over to get to their foe
But with clockwork fire they begin to slow

With a dent in the hammer, it comes to a halt
Despite greater numbers a failed assault
The Frenchman flees after an attack destined to fail
And stuck firmly between legs is the soldier's tail.

Iain Murray

Salute To Heroes

A single, solitary Spitfire stood on the ground
Three hours of training before it's skyward bound
I remember those times, that special engine roar
As I opened the throttle, I sat there in awe

Ten seconds that's all, to fly straight and true
Or you'll just boil the engine and that just won't do
Civilian spotters on radio, enemies on the way
They're now over Kent, time for them to pay

5,000 feet, 8,000 feet, 400 miles an hour
Looking for those bombers, horizon I now scour
At 20,000 feet they come into view, 100 plus bombers, I know what to do
303 bullets fire, 109 cannons blast
Battle in the skies as Luftwaffe flies past

Bombers in the clouds, some now in flames
Falling to the Thames, I'll never know their names
Time to turn around, wings need some repair
In twenty minutes' time I'll be back in the air

Hornchurch, Biggin Hill, Uxbridge and Kenley
276 pilots airborne, to fight along with me
Suppress those absent friends when the battle starts
Salute them all later with a pint and some darts

Battle raged for ten weeks, Hitler assured we'd fail
September 15th 1940, few lived to tell this tale
'This was our finest hour,' 'So much owed to so few'
Not for medal or thanks, remembrance will do.

Ian McAulay

Bring Him Back

I don't want stars.
I want back Father who
drove me to my new dorm
on my first day at university,
who linked up my TV and
computer and did all the electrical things only fathers can
do with a spark.

I don't want flags.
I want back Pops who
put glitter and shine up and
down the staircase on Christmas
Eve to make me believe in
something; like he wanted to
believe what *he* was doing was right.

I don't want hymns.
I want back Dad who
taught me to swim and dive for
pennies at the bottom of our local
pool and hold my breath, to not be
scared of what was beyond my
vision; his hair still dry somehow
even when under the surface.

I don't want stripes.
I even want back Dickhead who
I'd mouth at with surly disrespect
headed towards the telephone
because *he ruined absolutely everything
and totally understood nothing
about me whatsoever.*

I don't want the guard.
I want back Grandad who
loved early morning get-ups
again and was a soft touch for
sweets and chocolate and
who smiled more and more each
time he saw them running up
the driveway.

I don't want any of the things
that you're meant to have or should have
to respect, to remember and to not
forget.

I want *him* back.

Thomas Harrison

Weary With War

Into battle with weary limbs
Heavy in the cold, wet mud,
Ragged clothes on jagged skin,
Arms that would fight if they could.

Weak from injuries and hunger,
Trying now to quench the thirst,
With dread of unknown things to come
And fear that it may just get worse.

I'll write to my girlfriend later,
Tell her that I'm okay;
Without mention of the misery
There really won't be much to say.

Organised, prolonged destruction,
Sacrifices all the way,
Ruination and disruption,
Violence, when for peace I pray.

Jean Aked

Wasteland In The Slums

Bottom line with a black bag
starving on the
front line.
Mud-painted ankles
Flies quiver in the air –
No noise. Eerie silence
deadly smell.
A wound – torn on the surface – flesh
blood delves into
the fingerprints
cracks, an abandoned bird would shovel
around the conflict.
No calming calls for
a precious tit, bombs echo through the vacuum,
through time,
no one wants to move –
wants to sleep it away.
DNA left deep in land, grime,
rotting into history of
a patch
of
grass.
Years later,
as tourists explore.

Ryan Bremner-Wright

Crazy Roundabout

The six wise men
Stood on the hill
And observed the torn map
Facing them all

Maybe the disagreements would cease
As if they could agree on where they could land
Put simply, their cities, farms and forts
Sadly led to this

But as one man stated his case
Another quoted scripture
Solemnly swearing to defend his
Every move on the map
Defiant to the last

Comrades in arms
Over land and sea, come together
Next to one another, as
Foes share the same plot of
Land, argued over
In anger, not calm discussion
Creating a terrible
Toll of those lost.

Brian Francis Kirkham

Warfare

Blood-soaked, mud-splattered khaki, scattered all around,
Bodies, arms, legs, mired in a rat-infested morass,
Rocket flares overhead, illuminating the battleground,
Air, still sharp with the **lingering** stench of gas.

The relentless crump, crump of heavy guns nearby,
Silhouetting tanks and men with every flash,
Like cut-out figures, outlined against the sky,
They rally and regroup for one last dash.

Knowing nothing of warfare, they went with a brave heart,
Untrained boys and men, inexperienced officers leading,
Not enough ammunition, not enough men, doomed from the start,
Soon to be felled and left, dying, broken, bleeding.

Up from the trenches, heading for the wire,
A final attempt, while there's still enough men,
No sooner out than caught in the crossfire,
Mercilessly cut down as they advanced. What then?

Do we send out more to die?
Boost the numbers to no avail,
Join with others beneath a foreign sky,
Whatever the course we must not fail.

Kenneth Capps

A Prayer For Humanity

Please pray for humanity, as the world is living in insanity,
Tragically, the government is controlling a cult of personality.
Because they think that they have the authority,
Creating an image of only hostility, causing catastrophe,
Blaming religion and blasphemy.

Conflict between each other internationally,
People dying in vanity, every day brutality, every day bloodshed,
Caused by people who don't agree with equality.
So please stop ignoring the spiteful reality,
The corruption of society,
Abolishing the rights of humanity, the right to freedom and sanity.

Generations of manipulation, frustration, aggravation,
False allegations come down to lack of communication,
Fighting over different beliefs, only causing grief.
Hopelessly searching for relief,
But for certain, every single soul in this world prays for peace,
So either let's agree or agree to disagree, please.
Build new formations of world peace.

Rebekah Daisy Peck

World At War

Soldiers dying for our country,
Families are left behind,
A baby cries, he wants his dad,
But war is cruelly blind.

It doesn't think about their mother,
It doesn't think about their son,
It doesn't think about anyone,
As long as it's won.

We fight for our rights for freedom,
But war has no happy ending,
It's forever got us in its clasp,
Our futures forever pending.

War brings people together,
They vow to defeat the enemy,
But what about the lives we're losing,
For grief it has no remedy.

I watch the news and listen in dismay,
Another soldier is no more,
A family sat at home, not wanting confirmation,
Not wanting that knock on the door.

I cry when I think about our children,
What future may await them,
A scary world, full of hate,
So unaware of what's to come.

War is a word written in blood,
Its victims fall straight to its feet,
Innocent lives and loving families
Are forced to admit defeat.

Shannon Ricard

Returning – Beirut 1993

The *clunk* as wheels descended
Ears popped as the aircraft lost height
Eyes straining out of windows
To see the land far below
Coming closer into view

A gentle frizz of excitement
Familiar to any landing
Soft murmuring in different tongues
Hands clasping armrests
Or loved ones' hands

One bump, then two
The roaring of the engines in reverse
The forward thrust of deceleration

Parched land outside the windows
Gives way to sparkling blue
Pockmarked grey buildings
Battered French vehicles
'Welcome to Beirut'

Suddenly a tumult of applause
Cheering, clapping, happy voices
Grown men hugging and crying
Tears of joy running down beards
Women ululating and shouting

The exiles returning
Druze and Maronite, Sunni and Shiite
War-weary rivals and adversaries
United in joy and anticipation

Determined to rebuild
A land long loved from afar
Bringing hope for a nation
Impetus for reconciliation

Welcome to Lebanon!

David Babatunde Babatunde Wilson

To Those Boys Who Never Came Back

The Wellingtons and Lancasters warmed up on the various stations
the crews on standby, trying hard to control their misgivings and fears,
each young man on their airbase knowing that going by past operations
the next day meant parents somewhere being overwhelmed and in tears

The lonely journey across the North Sea in that deathly black, starlit sky
each man concentrating on his job and being part of his well-trained team
but knowing soon they would all be the target of the enemy below
and praying that this was part of some dreadful nightmare or bad dream

To the outside world, they were brave, fearless crews defending our land
it can never be measured the courage they showed in conquering their fear
and yet it is thanks to those brave crews and their indomitable spirit
that you and I can enjoy the freedom in this England that we hold dear.

While the politicians and armchair generals in their plush offices, sat
hoping that each of the dreadful bombing raids would go as planned
to them, though hard, the resulting loss of life was *par for the course*
for the last chance for England's freedom lay with the Bomber Command

So, to all those boys who never made it back and lie in some foreign land
war memorials throughout the world commemorate your names with pride
and since then, many more men have died in the relentless search for peace
joining you in the Lord's glory, marching with your comrades side by side.

Don Woods

Purple Triangles

A life-changing special event occurred in 1939
We declared war against the Nazis
They said, 'There's something about a soldier that is fine, fine, fine'.
God was said to be on the side of both parties
But, at the end of the day, who side was He really on?
And who were the victims of Hitler's persecution?
There were a few groups, including Jews, that this dictator picked on
Another was Jehovah's Witnesses, he showed little mercy to them
They were identified by a symbol, a triangle of purple colour
When they were incarcerated in his concentration camps
Where they shared brotherly love and support to each other
Studying the scriptures under the shade of the lamps
Hitler became Dalek-like, vowing to exterminate this 'brood'
He was adamant he couldn't tolerate them in his land
As they wouldn't fight for his cause or submit to his rules
As far as he was concerned, he had no choice but to have them banned
In his eyes, they were a group of traitors, up to no good
But they believed in obeying God rather than men
And they refused to worship idols made of stone or wood
And Hitler was the biggest idol in Germany back then
But what sort of example did he set those who admired him?
His days came to an end because he took his own life
He no doubt felt intimidated by those who conspired against him
In his final days before his mutual suicide with his wife.

Philip Dalton

House

I might have built a house,
Down by the old town. Now
My soul drowns and I see
Hopes in me wilt. Can't douse
The fires that burn and singe.
I'm cowering behind
Walls, wishing that an
Escape presents itself,
In this ruined landscape.
They'll hunt me, I won't
Make my house. It will
Remain unbuilt, in the recesses of my mind.
And bombs and shells
Will leave me blind.
I'll breathe my last, leaving
My fallen world behind.

Muhammad Khurram Salim

War

The windswept barren land
Shows soldiers with their guns in hand,
Alert to danger from the foe.
The day would come when they could go;
But for now they had to stand
Along the road to this war-torn land.
For all the men the days are long
Of fighting, shooting and the strong
Smell of putrefying bodies lying low,
Behind the inhuman barricade
Of defence tanks and bandages.
Oh weary men must all go home
One day, when peace is called,
And wounds are healed.
Buried are the dead in graves
Marked with just a cross.

Kathy McCaig

Pots Of Peace

Man, unworthy recipient of ocean-wrapped planet presented
Melting ice caps, polluted rivers, forests slashed and burning
Higher intelligence of lowest kind, ozone tears, war zone scars
Waging death, destruction, inevitable fanatical self-combustion
Against essence of religion turning, into terrorists converting
Power games, maximum score pain, high levels of human failings

Wake up! Shape up! Smile upon first verse snowdrops of spring
Opening lines of their opal set clusters makes heart ring
Glinting with morning dew, foliage carpet pushing through
Seeking sunlight to survive, in amity they blossom, thrive
Let humanity peep from beneath undergrowth layers deep
Use not abuse this bud of life, aim instead to be better, be kind

War, it changes nothing and yet everything, every thing
Habitat strangulation by knot weed ground force invasion
Potted olive branches plant in window boxes of tiny minds
From divided roots cultivation of new, unified, green shoots
Tentacle trails from propagation not propaganda, spread tales
Seeds of peace sow, into a better world they may grow.

Shirley Clayden

Man

Doesn't he know, can't he tell
If he goes on like this, then we will end up in Hell
Hasn't he learned from history past
That if he wants this world to last
Then he must put a stop to this terrible campaign
There really is nothing at all he can gain
Except for all that blood and loss of life
Thousands upon thousands and nothing but strife
And this is just because of his never-ending greed
That he wants *war* upon *war* – to succeed!
But doesn't he know, why won't he understand
This was all foretold, this was all planned
He is being manipulated and he is for hire
And the world will finally end in a *big ball of fire!*

Barbara Coward

A Dark Hour

As time drifts by
minute by minute, hour by hour
day by day
we sit watching the carnage unfolding
in front of our eyes
the wars tearing at the very fabric of society
apart from us, every day
wars ravaging the lands around us
intolerance and persecutions
running rife in the world's scope.
Innocents being slaughtered
as the women cry
the men stand with guns in hand, fighting
an endless war
A game of war that holds our futures
A game caused by dark forces
The ones in control of our destinies
stand in the mists of time.

Emma Hewitt

For The Love Of My Country

My dearest enemy
Have I angered you in some way
That you might hang me
Without discussion on this matter
By taking the law into your hands
Along with your deputies of hate?
For you are surely not a gentleman
All you achieve is to divide each social group with your propaganda
Placing fear where there may have been understanding
Persecuting those who choose to not believe in your lies

Only the Devil steals souls
Only true Christians possess true faith
Only the blind follow men of ignorance
Only thugs resort to violence

I take my faith with me wherever I go
For I am my own keeper
Without followers or believers
Surely if we adopted your ideals of classless society
Wouldn't this be communism?
Seeing as there are only a few countries left under this regime
Perhaps you'd be better off there
Oh, but you can't
For they have no state benefits like the ones we have in this country
Yet you're still not satisfied

There are no wages for martyrs
No supplements for the cause
No medals for the campaigners
Who choose to ignore the fact that people are indifferent
No Nobel prize for you my son
No remembrance service
Like the ones befitting our war heroes
Who saved this country from the likes of you

Maybe you don't realise what a great country this is
We all have the right to express ourselves
This is true and often abused
Did you feel the power
The rush of venom

As the bottle broke
Or was it all those years of being bullied at school
That finally made you snap?
Little boys' games
Played either by hypocrites or fools
Handing out leaflets with the purpose of shocking the opposition

Maybe it's just simply my blonde hair and blue eyes
Or the way I goose step around town
Perhaps it's that invisible SS uniform you always see me in
That makes me look German

For the love of my country
For the sake of my family and friends
I will not yield to such pressure
That would deny me my identity
For I am English and proud.

Patriotism is not racism.

Deadboy

Raw Truth

Reversing through the diminishing smoke,
spiralling upwards into the clouds.
Wings:
Reattach themselves.
The blazing inferno that had engulfed
them, snuffed out.
Explosions:
Harmonise with the low euphonious
drumming of propellers.
Fuselages:
Wounded, that bullets had ripped open,
heal.
Calm air:
Planes returning,
distant droning approaching,
runways, watching silently, waiting.
An end to all destruction.
Time racing back to peace.

Everything flying.
Everything fleeing.
Everything fluttering.

The fallen: Rise,
each life gifted back.
Prisoners escaping, running back
towards their starting point.
Sunken ships meander through torturous
currents, rising to the surface,
every sailor plucked from the sea,
returned safely to their ships.
Cold water droplets evaporating.

Everything standing.
Everything staring.
Everything still.

Zeros, possessed in their acceleration,
hurtling down towards the trembling ships.
Sailors' and pilots' eyes meet, hurling shards
of hate at each.

Guns shower all.
The roaring air; silenced.

A glitch in time.

The plane, grabbed by a hand
is flung, spinning high into the sky
Fading further and further away, fading, fading . . .

Severed arms and legs slither across
the slippery deck.
Shimmering blood refilling veins, wounds
and slashes healing.
Limbs reattaching.
Dirt, slime, debris disappearing.
Bullets search for their barrel.

Everything recovering.
Everything returning.
Everything reverting.

Doodlebugs lift,
breathing in their smoke.
Craters disappear.
Rubble rebuilds every house.
Coventry Cathedral rises,
like a phoenix from the ashes.
Melted stained glass,
mends.
Sun:
Illuminating,
beautiful colours.
An act of God.
Souls revive.
Sirens; fading, fading, fading . . .

Everything glowing.
Everything glimmering.
Everything glorious.

This is raw truth.
This is war.

Christabel Martin

In Cities And Towns

Atrocious, barbaric acts
The media displays the facts
Numerous lives shattered
Countless pints of blood splattered
Across cities and towns.

Fleeing migrants searching for new lives
Death comes to children, husbands and wives
Arguments and wrangling where they should go
And still innocent blood does flow
Across the world – in cities and towns.

Dreadful scenes
On our television screens
Debris on the ground
Mortars continue to pound
Cities and towns.

Children running away in fear
As craters in the soil appear
Families torn apart
The enemies have no heart
For those living in cities and towns.

Land covered by putrid plumes of smoke
Seeing a war zone is no joke
Scars will take years to heal
For the young and innocent I feel
Forced to leave cities and towns.

Men and women dying in battle
Slaughtered like cattle
Evil deeds perpetrated on one another
Sister killing sister – brother fighting brother
Across the land – in cities and towns.

Patricia J Tausz

We Were Not There

The holocaust, a disgrace, a tragedy
A blot on Mankind's page of history.
Millions of Jews, Romas, Witnesses,
Gays and the disabled killed.
Pictures of skeletal survivors
That was bad enough,
But we weren't there.
We have no idea of the truth.
Herded into ghettos
Only 200 calories a day to eat
From there onto cattle trucks
No better than animals
No food, water or privacy
But we weren't there.
The camps were even worse
Were they going straight
To the shower gas chambers
Or to be put to work in the camps
Or for 'medical research'?
Degraded beyond measure
But we weren't there.
Stripped, shaved, numbered
No identity, no individuals
Starved, beaten, worked to death
Filth and dirt the norm
No sanitary facilities here
Dehumanised and humiliated
But we weren't there.
How can we really know the truth
Words and pictures
They don't even begin to tell the story
The truth is out of our comfort zone
Their strength to survive amazing
How did anyone survive?
Thank God we weren't there.

Jaz

The World At War

My grandfather and his brother, Edward
Volunteered for the war
In World War One they served to its end
Both of them suffered in conditions quite hard
Then they died and suffered no more!
When the war didn't kill them the
Aftermath did and they disappeared
Through death's ever bleak door
They suffered in vain though they did their best
For their lives were lost in the ultimate test
For them, half of God's three score years and ten lives were lost
When they fought in the war, it was the ultimate cost!

Royston E Herbert

Coquelicots

When the autumn scythe had cut the last of the standing wheat,
When the broken land had been turned and tilled by human hand,
Winter came and held its icy grip as this land lost the last of its heat
And countless souls known to man were lost in that forsaken land.

In the pain of peace, we stayed, as silence intensified the grief,
When winter held no hope of life, as bereft as the frozen earth,
Then the wait was o'er as the vernal growth of myriad blade and leaf,
Came to renew our latent faith, as Nature gave her silent rebirth.

Then summer. Luscious with each gentle scent and welcome sight
And with her came coquelicots, blood-red against the clear blue sky
Swathe after swathe they danced in the breeze, brazen, free and bright,
No serried ranks ordered lines. Freely their petals did fly.

As I gaze o'er this land and contemplate their delicate forms
I see them,
I remember them,
Coquelicots, here to remind us all,
Poppies come,
Flower, then fall.

M A Baker

War-Torn Heartstrings

A world at war surrounds us
Not merely in catastrophically war-torn peacetime
But in the human heart
Battlefield of good and evil

As poison plots and shoot-out fever resound
In many streets and public places
With ambiguity and confusion
As to what a public conscience actually is

News items reflecting the scene, as observed by a casual bystander
As an old lady is shot in a care home
And international terrorism brings fear to English shores

The world is truly at war, internally and externally
In seemingly shameless pervasion of homicidal mania
So who can put a stop to it?
Anyone at all, before the final whistle blows on a tragic tour
Across a libertine showground?

Tracy Allott

Remembering The War

For I was only six years old
The war years, many stories told
A bomb was dropped onto our home
So we lost everything we owned
We moved to somewhere safe and then
Such happy days we often spent
You never had to lock your doors
For no one wanted what was yours
We never went without you know
And Mother worked her magic so
We always had good things to eat
And once a month had sweets, a treat
And at the end of the war years
We had street parties, loads of cheer
I guess we look back fondly to
The memories I've shared with you.

Jeanette Gaffney

Shock And Awe (Full Circle)

I crossed the sea with Moses
and we smote the Medianites.
We slaughtered the entire race
and set their cities all alight.
Moses turned to me and said,
'We must strike with shock and awe.'
I said, 'Is that what God commands?'
He said, 'What else are young men for?'
and it makes me weep
that life's so cheap
we squander it on war.

I followed Alexander
and we conquered many lands.
in the Indus we did wash away
the blood that stained our hands.
We fought with bow and sword and shield
and left our dead upon the earth.
I said, 'Please tell me Alexander
is this all that life is worth?'
Alexander answered me,
'What else are young men for?'
and it makes me weep
that life's so cheap
we squander it on war.

I marched with Caesar's legions
from Caledonia to Rome.
We conquered more than half the world
and then we went back home.
We left behind a bloody trail
a thousand thousand lost.
I turned and said to Julius,
'Was it really worth the cost?'
And Julius did answer me,
'What else are young men for?'
and it makes me weep
that life's so cheap
we squander it on war.

Now I fought alongside Constantine
at the battle of Milvian Bridge
and the dead did pile up one more time
like ghosts upon the ridge.
By this sign we did conquer
a cross painted with gore.
'Tell me Constantine,' I said
'Must we kill for evermore?'
And Constantine did answer me,
'What else are young men for?'
and it makes me weep
that life's so cheap
we squander it on war.

Next I rode with Genghis Khan
to fight the dreaded Chin.
We crossed the wall and killed them all
and then we sacked Peking
and so I said To Genghis
'Was it really worth the price?'
And he turned around and said to me,
'It's just the turning of the dice,
but if you really have to know,
'What else are young men for?'
And it makes me weep
that life's so cheap
we squander it on war.

I travelled with The Lionheart
to take back the Holy Land
and at the sack of Acre
we slaughtered out of hand
whether Mussulman or Christian
no quarter was ever shown.
'Don't worry,' Good King Richard said,
'For God will know his own.'
Then he turned and said to me,
'What else are young men for?'
And it makes me weep
that life's so cheap
we squander it on war.

I rode alongside Bonaparte
from Moscow to the Nile
many comrades lost the heart
to march another mile,
they shouted, 'Vive la Emperor'
and sang La Marseillaise,
they followed on the eagle's heels
and sang Ol' Boney's praise
then Napoleon turned and said to me
'What else are young men for?'
And it makes me weep
that life's so cheap
we squander it on war.

Then I stood beside the Kaiser
in the greatest war of all,
the cannons rang, the bullets sang
and we watched the young men fall.
Thirty thousand dead men,
on the first day of the Somme.
'Tell me Wilhelm,' I said to him,
'Don't you feel that this is wrong?'
He turned around and said to me,
'What else are young men for?'
And it makes me weep
that life's so cheap
we squander it on war.

Barely twenty years had passed
and off I went again,
this time the raging war was fought
with tank and ship and plane.
Thousands more were slaughtered
as death rained from the air.
'Tell me Adolf, my old friend,
is it true that you don't care?'
And Adolf turned and said to me,
'What else are young men for?'
And it makes me weep
that life's so cheap
we squander it on war.

The next time that I went to war in farway Iraq
it was Bush and Blair who sent us there
then stabbed us in the back.
the campaign we embarked upon
Bush called 'shock and awe'
and something deep inside me said,
I've been here once before.
I said to Tony, 'Can you tell me the reason for the war?'
Then I saw his eyes and knew he lied,
but
'What else are young men for?'

Nigel Sinclair

The Father In Me!

(The Paris Attacks November 19th 2015)

I the person the protector,
A man
Of opposite and equal sides,
The funny conflictions of my own selfish pride
Putting them on the backburner,
What I truly want is my babies to be happy,
Safe
Free to not worry about
Crime 'n' terror,
In our mitts the graphic terror-wrists.
Holding hands,
I fear, my fear fi foe the time that I bestow,
I've got to go!
Bleeding buildings an pavement aside
The nation's blood Runneth over a cup with no sides,
Nobody hears their sobbing cries
I hear a little voice say, 'Daddy will they kill us will they come here? '
Reassurance runs deep within their little hearts we keep.
We reply, 'The candles burn bright as your guiding angel light,
So to keep us safe from harm, hold us in our loving father's arms
Hold us safe keeps us clear from danger that is near'.
Amen.

Paul Blair

World At War

Wars are not won . . .
Everyone loses
Death is the winner
Of each one it chooses

Mangled and torn,
Brave soldiers lay dying
What's it all for?
They seem to be crying

Wars are fought . . .
Whether lost or won
Our young soldiers die
Their lives are gone

Loved ones weep . . .
The days are long
Their vigils keep
Their hopes prolonged

Now white crosses stand
Row upon row
Each holding memories
That we'll never know

Sylvia Gawler

Untitled

I walked among a field of poppies
to see what I could see,
rising up from the soil were souls of vibrant green.

They hovered around the silent ground,
never able to make a sound,
quivering when they heard the toll of the old church bell,
for it reminded them of their funeral knell . . .

Dips where trenches once laid,
echoes from clanging blades,
for those few survivors the bloody memories never fade.

Flanders Field, a field of pain,
that no amount of years could ever sway.

Still we march on rejoicing in our freedom
living with the vain hope that they reached the golden kingdom.

Lest we forget the selfless sacrifices they made,
lest we forget the price they courageously paid
for it was never theirs to pay,
War will never wait for Judgement Day.

War sows poisonous seeds and eradicates harmony
leaving us in powerless silence,
mourning those heroes we never knew
and those surviving bearing a guilty medal for their dues.

A piece of brass will not bring back their fallen friends
and how can we be sure they will reunite at the end?

Wars can never be won,
they can only escalate until no more damage can be done,
so they will never cease because scars never heal,
therefore I fear we will see many more Flanders Fields.
The threat we face is very real.

Until then, we will remember them
and thank them for all the peaceful years they fought for,
till another war will take its place,
so those souls no longer leave a trace.

I once walked among a field of poppies
to see what I could see,
but all there was were countless stones covered in weeds of mossy green,
withered red petals scattered across the ground
and the sound of crying, but no one was there to make a sound . . .

Olivia Todd

Thanks, Grandie Survived All WWI Battles

He told me of the nightmare clashes
He focused on the Somme, Passchendaele
From all the others
He enthused the buildings of France and Belgium
He was pleased at my British history at university
Although not war analysis, for which he was grateful
His post 1918 life was always talked of
The skill as engineer
Transferred through all coalfield ranks to manager
Across the country
He strode, although his heart was in his Nottinghamshire birthplace
As was my maternal granny
Both knew Byron's Newstead Hall Base
They both gave me happiness
With all things that happened concerning words.

Christopher Brookes

The War

My thought on war
it must be done for the more,
no matter how far or at our door,
we will do what we have to do now,
next week, next month, next year, next century.
Whenever. We will have to come together to make a nothing of this something.
Though, through past and at interjection.
We shall prove our reconciliation.
Always which we have.
The United Kingdom of Great Britain. England, Scotland, Northern Ireland and Wales,
Our royalist family have proven . . . through . . . and great promise.

We have amended, commended, celebrated, paid with poppies . . . sent letters to lobbies,
commons and common . . .

We stand at attention.

Jermaine Moore

Requiem

I heard a crash of thunder, that blew my mind asunder.
A voice called out my number on the last day of my life.
Lightning pierced my vision, images in collision
That danced in wild derision on the shadows of my life.
I smelled the stench of hatred, as bomb blast clouds abated
That turned my lungs to paper, one September of my life.
Glass splintered all around me, girders crushed and bound me.
Timbers warped and bound me and bled me of my life.
Warm blood oozed and soaked me, dust clouds cloaked and choked me
Screams of terror haunted me in the nightmare that was my life.
I didn't kiss my lover, I didn't hug my brother,
I didn't thank my parents for their precious gift of life.
I pray for peace in this land, I pray for peace in their land.
I place myself in God's hand to guide me through the night.
And when it dawns tomorrow, there'll be no grief or sorrow
But empty skies, ploughshares, requiem and Bach.
Resurgam.

David Birtwistle

Soldiers Of Peace

Why us? Why them?
Alone they depart, together as men.
Silently travelling the road unknown.
Loudly their hearts beat, aching for home.
Vacant eyes and lying smiles,
Adorn the faces as they march the miles.
The battle for their lives up over the hill,
Too scared to die, but afraid to kill.
A pointless fight, an endless war.
The way of man, is this what life is for?

Christopher Jenkins

Practise What You Preach

Bombs are dropped in the dead of night
Their impact is shown at the break of light
Only cowards fight the weak
Only monsters give no thought to the havoc they wreak
I was taught many moons ago
Two wrongs don't make a right
Perhaps these world leaders
Missed that day in school
Education fights terrorism
Inclusion fights alienation
Bombs create more wars
Whole villages burn brighter than the stars
Blowing up babies at Ground Zero
Killing the weak doesn't make you a hero
Media bias encourages attacks
It triggers a new influx of terrorist attacks
A picture speaks a thousand words
Take heed, you creators of evil
You who sells arms to the devil
And then takes umbrage when the devil strikes back
Stop killing innocent civilians for your own heinous creation
By bombing more settlements, you create more crisis
And play right into the hands of your creation, ISIS
If you want world peace
Practise what you preach

Asma Khatun

Homefront

I woke to the sound of a piercing scream
Thinking I was still in the throes of an unsettling dream
A morning sun and smoke-black skies
On the television, my home I couldn't recognise

She says we have lost the shopping mall
The park just rubble and so too the school
The street is littered with bricks, clothes and toys
I suddenly think of next-door's boys

The regular TV show has gone
A foreign newsman talking so forlorn
Recalling statistics crunched from human cost
The desperate, dead, angry and lost

One day, maybe one, I could return home
When the world has forgotten my town's name
When we are consigned to the history annals
And the world will go on the same

So you say this is different? A war to end war?
That this settles matters and it won't come to this anymore?
Yes. It's perverse that I am smiling at this
How many times have we heard all this before?

Stephen Prout

Four Inches Of Ground, For A Life

On those bright, sunny mornings, in those cold dark nights, the men in trenches paid it,
Through July, August, September, October, on into November we paid it . . .
And our families paid it too.

Artillery, snipers, trench raids, gas,
Grenades, mines and diseases,
Shelling, mortars, fights hand to hand and machine guns,
Always the machine guns . . .
Scorched by flamethrowers, buried in bunkers and drowned in endless mud,
Oh yes, we paid it . . .
And our families paid it too.

The bill came by telegrams, short, to the point.
'His Majesty regrets . . .'
Not nearly as much as those opening with trembling hand and watering eyes the envelopes,
Whose contents they knew but still dreaded to read.
But the bill still came, unannounced and unwelcome.
They paid it
As we had paid on the Somme.

And what of the commanders?
The generals who planned it?
The officers who led it?
What was their share of the 'Blood price of freedom?'
At night, every night, in their sleeping mind's eye an eternal parade . . .
The wounded, the missing, the dead and the dying.
Stretchers and coffins, in perfect formation, roll past in an endless parade of the damned.
For those who planned the campaign, no strategic withdrawal,
Just the sightless eyes of the long-since departed, gazing in silent reproach.
In their own way, the commanders paid it too.

And what of the businessmen, the bankers, the arms dealers?
Doing deals in money, in votes and in blood,
Watching the bloodshed and counting their profits so far from the guns and the dead strewn
in mud.
They seldom saw action, they seldom heard gunfire,
Not for them were the sights and the smells and the sounds.
Of limited conscience and stunted humanity, their guilt cast aside like the dead on the
ground.
It cost *them* nothing . . .

Mark Scantlebury

World At War

An eye for an eye makes the whole world blind,
Why can't people see the words they're spitting are not kind.
If they stopped focusing on what makes us all so different,
Maybe everyone would be just a little bit more tolerant.

If they stopped and listened, really listened to what they say,
Stopped lying and abusing and kept their own fears at bay,
The world would begin to look a little bit better,
And the tear-stained faces of the children wouldn't get wetter.
Perhaps then, we could start to have true and inner peace for all.
It would be a start, no matter how intensely small.

If only they could see,
They're not so different from you or me,
That all of us are broken, all of us are hurt,
Then maybe we could finally rebuild this world up from the dirt.
We're broken in every corner, not just one part,
This war between all people is breaking every heart.
So if we all just stopped, stopped and took a breath,
Maybe there would be just a little bit less death.

Verity Martin

Fear Across The Nation

Fear across the nation,
The hate engulfs your heart,
I pray for peace and forgiveness,
Let's not get up in arms.
Your fear controls your actions,
The hurt that you will cause,
Innocents are being lost,
While idiots applaud.
I pray that God will show you love,
And that we can be free,
To wipe out all extremist hate,
Where it may be.

Abbie Dixon

Go To Flanders

Go to Flanders
Your memory wanders
To a different age
Battles of fear, death and rage.
Here the blood-red poppies grow
Who's buried here we'll never know
Enemies amongst lines
Endless mines
Explosive gunfire
A sea of barbed wire
Guns and tanks
Know no ranks
Here men prayed
It was their last days
Now all is at peace
And enemies cease
Here the blood-red poppies grow
Who's buried here we'll never know.

Isabel Taylor

It Is Now

To readily say the words as quick as English weather changes
Is inhumane
To sentence a platoon of men to expected death
Is harrowing
But that is what he did
'You're over the top at 6am, get them ready'
Just like that he served his warrant
In just a few short hours we will face the lingering ghost
The shadow that has long reigned over us for so many long winters
This day is not an uncommon occurrence
For I have seen this many a time before
And I have never envied the braves ones
We wait . . . oh we wait . . . and wait
Until our number is called
A game of chance
It is like the chiefs are giants . . . standing over us with a pair of dice
Deciding who to send next
When we are called
Ghostly faces cling to every hope
Of survival
Their nail-bitten, wind-scalded hands clasp tightly onto a rifle
That would never even fire a shot
There would be no time
As they stand by the rickety ladder
Letters and last words pass to those staying behind
In the hope, that beyond the grave, words will reach loved ones
When the surface is breached, bullets like rain pour down
Until there is a river of blood
It feels like we are mere spiders being washed down a plughole
It is only when the rain stops that we can clamber up again
But then we are no longer alive
We are free
Free from warfare, free from bloodshed, free from the carcass of mud
We are the statistics you will read about
We are the pictures of courage who fought for this country

Many of us . . .
Are the unmarked man
We are the shadows of time
We are frozen
We are immortalised.

Emma Maskell

War Or Peace?

Why do we go to war
And put our lives in others' hands
Why do we invade countries?
That's something I just don't understand

We act as if war is the answer
That violence is the perfect solution
Our children are seeing poor examples
Creating more mayhem and dissolution

I may be a pacifist
I'm not afraid to say so
For what purpose does war solve
Causing death to others I don't know?

Call me a coward, call me a wimp
But I believe there is a better way
I pray one day we will realise
That it is love that will save the day

So many innocent people are killed
Yet we see this as sheer victory
And then we try to promote peace and love
Which I think is pure hypocrisy

What purpose does war solve
But only more bloodshed and pain?
Unless something changes today
History will repeat itself again.

Franklin Brady

War. War. War.

War, war, war,
It's everywhere we go,
Everywhere I look,
Soldiers come and go,
When will they come back?
An answer we'll never know,
Or will their names be left,
On a shiny, silver plaque,
To keep them in our memory,
To honour what they fought for,
To go down in history?

War, war, war,
Just what is it,
That they are fighting for?
From past times and new times,
There's always been a war,
Many different ones,
But war is all the same,
All the blood and guns,
It's such a nasty shame,
That we can't live in peace,
To make friends instead of enemies,
To love instead of hate,
But it's always been like this,
It's just a human trait,
And that is why we must live this way,
We must live with,
War, war, war.

Lucy-May Baker

Crash And Burn

One day the Earth will crash and burn into dust and rubble
And we'll stand watching from our broken homes as it all just crumbles
Second by second the tables slowly turn
And the vortex is twisting fate, trying to make it work
But only hope is left to salvage something pure
And what's left of the world will be for the rich, not the poor
It's not World War Three, it's just nuclear war
The end of us all, this is the fall.

The world's filled with evil, sadness, leaders and lies
Heaven's filled with the good ones who didn't survive and fell victim
To these victimless crimes
Oh, you criminal masterminds, what do you have in mind?
This world's only set for one thing
Kings and queens and girls who only want one thing
So break the mould while you still can, young man
And take all the glory with your own bare hands
Believe in you and make a stand
Be what you set out to be, have a plan
And never stop chasing that thing that makes you, you
After all, the world's ending. What you gonna do?

Billy Simms

1914

Men in the trenches briefly knew peace
on Christmas Day 1914.
Both sides agreed that fighting should cease -
they'd meet on the land in-between.

From no-man's-land they moved all the dead,
then offered a Christmas greeting.
Guns fell silent: there were songs instead
at this Anglo-German meeting.

In time, suspicion gave way to trust -
Christmas puddings and beer were shared.
Then in that foul, fearsome Flanders dust
their football prowess was compared.

The kicking began; the match was on -
Britons and Germans competed.
Just for a day all hatred was gone,
no matter who was defeated.

Where this took place a monument stands
and its aim is to introduce
the young to friendship of rival bands
and *'The Khaki Chums' Christmas Truce'.*

Janet Turner

Remembrance Day

Today we bow our heads in remembrance of those we lost.
Those who in wars their lives it did cost.
For the ones who fought for us to survive.
Through the hardship and hard times they did strive.
Today marks the memorial of all the people laid to rest.
Today the poppy will be emblazoned on your chest.
Today brings sorrow and happiness in one emotion.
Today is about those who showed such devotion.
RIP and may your deaths not have been in vain.
God gained so many angels and the families felt the pain.
Today is respected by so many and felt in different ways.
As the memorials begin to get a load of bouquets.
The heads begin to bow down and thoughts fill the mind.
To what horrors and fights these men and women were confined.
Today is about them and understanding the fight for our existence.
Today is understanding there was no line of least resistance.
So God bless the many women and men who passed in these dreadful wars.
This will not be a day anyone ignores.

Shannon Fountaine

My Favourite War

Always men need to create tombs
how many times
tissues for the lie
blow remembrance of the pain
and when a war has triumphed
and put its dead on view
it is time for loading a tomb
to complete laying
the production of battle glory
a worn badge denoting the war adage

For British failure buckets of pain
a hail of blood
with us idiots and you
and all of it going down the drain.

Simon Warren

News At Ten

Urgent, imperative title music
Announces the start of News at Ten;
Seated in studio, at automatic cameras
World events read aloud by good-looking men.

Footage reveals appalling carnage
Buildings and bodies shattered and torn
Faces of terror, hunger and torture
Faces of women who can only mourn.

Jangling, discordant noises of battle
Kalashnikovs, rockets, automatic machines
Houses in tatters, refugees fleeing
From unspeakable acts – things most obscene.

Reporter reveals Eastern Europe in crisis -
The TV shows all in its flickering light
We watch and we listen and raise not a finger
To lessen the hardship of our brothers' plight.

Informed by the details of how others suffer
We continue our viewing dispassionately;
Not callous, but powerless to stop needless slaughter
So what is the use of broadcast TV?

Margaret Cassidy

Heroes One And All

Some left home as boys
And some came home as men
Some left home as boys
But never came home again
Some left home as boys
To answer their country's call
Some left home as boys
But heroes one and all.

George David Hope

Forward Poetry Information

We hope you have enjoyed reading this book - and that
you will continue to enjoy it in the coming years.

For free poetry workshops please visit **www.forwardpoetry.co.uk**.
Here you can also join our online writing community 'FP
Social' and subscribe to our monthly newsletter.

Alternatively, if you would like to order further copies of this book or any
of our other titles, then please give us a call or log onto our website.

Forward Poetry Information
Remus House
Coltsfoot Drive
Peterborough
PE2 9BF

(01733) 890099